Michele A

Hope

"TO TRUST"

21 Day Devotional

In His Grace Ministries LLC

Dedication

To anyone who is in need of a gentle reminder of hope, God's hope.
May He speak to you through these words and may you feel His presence
always.

He

is our

hiding

place

YOU ARE MY REFUGE AND MY SHIELD;
I HAVE PUT MY HOPE IN YOUR WORD.
PSALM 119:114

Day 1

My refuge and my shield, other translations use the words You are my hiding place and my shield. My grandbaby likes to play a game she lovingly calls monster. It's essentially a ramped-up version of hide and seek. Mind you, she is 2.5 years old with an imagination as far as you can see. She loves to engage with and connect with you on a level I can't say I have seen with any other toddler, and no, I am not being biased, haha. She is as sharp as a tack and quick as a whip. In her game of monster, two of us run around screaming, in a good way, if screaming can be good; while the other chases after us. We then hide behind a door, cover ourselves with blankets or pillows, or whatever is around, holding tight onto one another as we wait. The other person runs after us and seeks us out. "Are you in the living room? No, not there. Are you in the playroom? No, not there." All the while those of us hiding try to be quiet, but instead hold our fingers up to our mouths and say "shh", trying not to laugh. We hold the pillows up as a shield so we can't be seen. The one seeking says "roar" once they have found the others. When they find us we scream and laugh and start the game all over again. She loves this and we will run for hours, hiding, screaming, running, and laughing. She trusts us. She has faith in us that we will run to the ends of the earth for her and with her. She knows in her heart of hearts that we will never let her down, not intentionally anyway. And she loves us. Why does she trust us so much? Because she hears our voices, she listens to our words. She knows who we are. She spends time with us, getting to know who we are as her grandparents.

Isn't this much like the Lord with us? We trust Him. Because we hear His voice, we listen to His words. We know who He is. We spend time with Him, getting to know who He is as our Heavenly Father. He is our hiding place. A place for us to run to. A place where we are safe. Sometimes when we run, we are screaming and sometimes we are laughing. Needing His arms around us as we wait in silence, holding our finger up to our mouth saying "shh". The day seemingly too hard to bear.

Or perhaps when we hide, we hide with a friend who will sit there with us and hold on tight. And when the time is right, you either laugh or scream or both. Because that is where life has taken you. Both of you waiting. Waiting for the "roar" to come. Waiting on God. *"Wait for the Lord; be strong, and let your heart take courage; wait for the Lord!"* Psalm 27:14. He will find you right where you are at. You wait for Him to gather you up in His arms and hold you. But in the waiting, you continue to seek Him and you peek; you peek out from under that blanket; you peek out from behind the pillow, keeping your eyes on Him. Because you know that He is where your help comes from. He is your refuge, your hiding place. And you remember that He is right there with you as you huddle underneath your pillow.

He should be the one we run to first and the most often. God sees our greatest joys, our biggest laughter, and He sees our painful tears and our hugest, biggest mistakes, and failures. And the failures of others towards us. But He is our refuge, our hiding place. He loves us because He knows us. He knows what is in the deepest parts of our hearts. He forgives, and He forgets, and He waits with arms open wide for us to run into them.

How do we gain this trust, His refuge, and shield? We read His Word. We listen. We get to know who He is. We take the time to be with Him. Our hope, our trust, is in His Word. In what He says. We trust in His promises. God shields us from the fiery arrows,. In fact, He protects us at all times. *"You are my refuge and my shield; I have put my hope in Your Word"*

Notes

Pray

Arm

yourself

with God's

Word

BUT IN YOUR HEARTS REVERE CHRIST AS LORD. ALWAYS BE PREPARED TO GIVE AN ANSWER TO EVERYONE WHO ASKS YOU TO GIVE THE REASON FOR THE HOPE THAT YOU HAVE. BUT DO THIS WITH GENTLENESS AND RESPECT,

1 Peter 3:15

Day 2

Hope

"TO TRUST"

Just like peace, our hope comes from the Lord. He is our source and giver of hope. Genuine hope. Our trust, placed in Him.

In 1 Peter 3:8-17 Peter is telling us that when we suffer from evil, we are not to retaliate back. He says, *"Do not repay evil with evil or insult with insult. On the contrary, repay evil with blessing"* v.9. We are to love and pray for our enemies, Matthew 5:44, which is so different from what the world tells us, isn't it? When someone hurts you you hurt them back. When someone says something false about you you say something back. The list goes on. But God's way is different. He is teaching us to have compassion and love for those who persecute and try to do all sorts of harm against us. It's not always easy. Trust me. I can say truthfully that I have had first-hand experience with people lying about me. With people who have threatened me. It's a hard place to be in. But if we look in the right place, it can be filled with peace and with hope. With the right heart, you can turn around and say "I will pray for that person". Don't get me wrong, there are times when the fleshly side wants to say something, but you pause, you think better of it and you move forward with a heart like Jesus. And you pray. You speak words of kindness over that person and you hope in the future that they will make better decisions themselves.

In v.13 Peter says, *"Who is going to harm you if you are eager to do good?"* *"But"* Peter goes on to say. Meaning there's more to this. There is more that can and will happen. *"But even if you should suffer for what is right, you are blessed. "Do not fear their threats; do not be frightened."* v.14. Blessed? Blessed within evil, blessed within suffering? When we stand up for the cross it seems foolish to some. But we are to rejoice, rejoice in the knowledge that if we are persecuted because of Jesus, it means that the Spirit of God rests on us. It means that we are heading in the right direction. Don't lose sight of the goal. Don't lose sight of who God is. We are not to fear how others act or have a fear of what others say. People will notice the difference in you. Some might not understand it and will try to goad you into a response or action. Others will want what you have. In either situation, you need to be prepared. Arm yourself with God's Word. Arm yourself with His knowledge and His example. Be prepared. Be honest. Be gentle and kind, full of respect. Cling to the blessing and cherish the peace and the hope found within you.

Notes

You,

Lord, are

our refuge,

our hiding

place

Guide me in
Your truth
and teach me,
for You are
God my Savior,
and my hope
is in You
all day long.

Psalm 25:5

Day 3

Hope
"TO TRUST"

David, a man after God's own heart, found himself in many precarious situations. We see him lament time and time again throughout the Psalms. He seeks after God in each of these situations. He cries out to Him, begging God to rescue him from his enemies, from those trying to do him harm. We see David praise God and even remind God of His promises. We see David be honest with God in how he is feeling. He expresses himself openly with our Heavenly Father, knowing that God would bend down and listen.

We see David start Psalm 25 in a state of worship, of surrender in prayer. David is pressing in. Much like he had done in the past. He prays that God would not put him to shame or allow his emeries to triumph over him, v.2. David is afraid, he doesn't want his enemies to prevail. He continues on *"No one who hopes in you will ever be put to shame"* v.3, we see this same sentiment repeated by Paul in a letter to the Romans. *"Hope does not put us to shame..."* 5:5. Oh this sweet hope, trust in the Lord. That when our faith is placed in who God is He will protect us, He will wipe away any guilt or shame that we might be carrying. David was no stranger to sin. David messed up many times in many ways. But God was faithful, and David was faithful to God. Often crying out, often surrendering himself to the One who holds it all. David was asking God to show him how to act and react to those around him. David was asking God to teach him His truth. David was asking for guidance within his situation. "Guide me, teach me" David cries. Lead me, Lord, my hope, my trust is in You.

This is where we should find ourselves when life is pushing on us from all sides. When our enemies are attacking on every side. When our situations are less than optimal. We should surrender ourselves in a state of worship and prayer. In honesty, we should cry out to the Lord, guide me, teach me Your ways. Show me how I am to act and react. Lord, I put my trust in You, forever and always. My hope is in You, Lord. Help us remember Your promises. You, Lord, are our refuge, our hiding place. Just like David, we have confidence that You will rescue us and protect us because our hope is in You.

Notes

Our anchor

of hope

is tethered to

the heavens

We have this hope as an anchor for the soul, firm and secure. It enters the inner sanctuary behind the curtain,

HEBREWS 6:19

Day 4

Hope
"TO TRUST"

Having the ability to anchor a boat is very important. From having the right equipment to its proper usage. The chain attached to the anchor must be of excellent quality, if you buy an inexpensive chain it will more than likely break when the strong currents come. You must also know where to throw your anchor and how far, as your boat will drift from side to side. Once your anchor is dropped this doesn't mean that your work is done. You have to be diligent in tying off your anchor and checking your reference points often. Regularly using your compass to make sure you have not drifted off.

In the early church and the ancient world, an anchor was a symbol of hope. Our hope is our anchor. Our hope is in Christ. Even in the fiercest of storms, our anchor, our hope will hold us firmly. Our boat might sway, and water might spill in from all sides, but God is there. Much the same as a boat's anchor, when the seas get rough and the storms surround us, we cast our anchor into the unseen. It firmly attaches itself to the seafloor. Finding something strong enough to hold tight to. Our anchor of hope is tethered to the heavens. Our anchor of hope should lead us directly to our Heavenly Father. Our chain is Jesus, interconnected with the Holy Spirit. Nothing and no one can take Him away from us. We are steadfast, firmly placed in Him.

Make sure that your foundation of hope is solid, is firm. Your relationship with Jesus directly affects your relationship with our Heavenly Father. John 14:6; *"Jesus answered, "I am the way and the truth and the life. No one comes to the Father except through me."* To be securely fashioned, you need to stay in the Word. You need to maintain your faith and knowledge. Because when the storms come, you will need to draw from the well of knowledge. The knowledge of who Christ is. His promises to us and the peace that we can have right smack dab in the middle of a storm.

Through Jesus' death and resurrection, we have been allowed behind the curtain. We have been allowed into the sweet presence of God. Nothing better, nothing purer.

Notes

His

name is

Jesus

I wait for the Lord, my whole being waits, and in His Word I put my hope

Day 5

There is an ache in your heart so deep you never thought you would experience relief. This ache, this heartbreak courses through your body, unrelenting to your cries. When will it end? When will you see the light?

The Psalmist is feeling these same feelings. *"Lord, hear my voice. Let your ears be attentive to my cry for mercy."* Psalm 130:2. He is asking God to listen. He is asking God to have mercy on him. But the Psalmist knows. He understands God's mercy and forgiveness. And he decides instead of staying in this place, he places his hope in the Lord. *"I wait for the Lord, my whole being waits"* He is placing himself into God's hands. He is willing to stop and rest a moment. He is willing to listen to the Words that God will speak. And God can speak in many ways. In the gentle whisper of the wind as it passes by. The flutter of a butterfly as it gently lands beside him. The wise counsel from a dear friend. He waits. He trusts. He listens.

We can sometimes forget to listen. We pray, we read, we write, we fill in the blank, and then we move forward with our day. Forgetting that God wants to talk to us. Forgetting to wait for a response to our cries.

Oh, sweet ones, if you have found yourself in a place such as this, know that there is light in the darkness. His name is Jesus. Grab hold of Him today. He is reaching out to you. He is running to you as you look up to Him. Don't despair. Don't forget to listen. And don't forget to wait on Him and put your hope in Him today.

Notes

Our strength

is not

our own

Isaiah 40:31

but those who hope
in the Lord
will renew their
strength. They will
soar on wings like
eagles; they will
run and
not grow weary,
they will walk
and not be faint.

Day 6

Hope
"TO TRUST"

Have you ever had a time when you thought you couldn't go on? You felt almost paralyzed with where you were at in life. The punches just keep coming and you can barely lift your head up off of your pillow in the morning and go about your day. You would much rather lay your head back down and pull the covers up over your head. I mean like far up over your head, so the light can't get through. Your eyes can't see what is around you. Wishing for sleep to take away the hurt and the pain. To take you away for a few precious moments where you can forget all that is going on.

Perhaps you have forgotten to look up and not out. To look up into the heavens and rest your weary eyes and heart on the Lord. Instead of looking out into your circumstances. Forgetting that you don't have to worry or fear about what is surrounding you.

Isaiah says, *"Do you not know? Have you not heard? The Lord is the everlasting God, the Creator of the ends of the earth. He will not grow tired or weary, and His understanding no one can fathom. He gives strength to the weary and increases the power of the weak."* 40:28-29

Do you not know, have you not heard? God never grows tired or weary. He constantly watches over you. He constantly extends His strength to those who are weary and weak. To those whose trust and hope are in Him. He provides. He cares. He listens. He understands. He loves.

Isaiah goes onto say: *"but those who hope in the Lord will renew their strength."* Our strength is not our own. It comes from God; God does not expect us to navigate this world by ourselves. But He requires us to place our hope in Him. To actively participate. *"They will soar on wings like eagles"* we will take on His strength in order to rise above our circumstances. *"they will run and not grow weary, they will walk and not be faint"* in Him, our strength never fades. In Him, trust and hope take on a whole new meaning. We do not have to do this on our own. We rely on God and what He provides for us.

We remember that at any moment all we have to do is cry out to the Lord and He will hear. He will renew our strength, we will soar on wings like eagles, we will run and not grow weary, we will walk and not be faint.

Notes

If we

never suffer

we never

learn

to trust

May those who
fear You
rejoice when
they see me,
for I have
put my hope
in Your Word.

Day 7

Hope
"TO TRUST"

The psalmist is praying to God to direct his steps. To teach him. To make his eyes look upon God's goodness and His Word instead of drifting and settling on worldly, worthless things. Preserve my life, he cries, for my comfort is in You. Even when others mock him. Even when they bind him and lie about him. He says he will meditate on God's Word. But he wonders when God will step in and comfort him. Never losing his faith or trust in who God is or in His promises. He was always learning, meditating, and seeking after God. Trusting that God's Word would be a lamp unto his feet and a light to his path. We can see that the Psalmist is going through some tough trials with others. They seem to come at him from all sides, not letting up, pursuing him, and his heart is about at the point of all he can take. But he keeps reminding himself of who God is. Of God's promises. Continually calling on the Lord. Continually placing his hope, his trust in who God is. Deliver me, he cries. Deliver me from my suffering, I haven't forgotten Your Word. Defend and redeem me, preserve my life. My heart trembles at Your Word, my heart stands in awe of Your Word, the Psalmist says. Imagine having this much faith and hope that you would still stand in awe of God and His Word when others are pressing inward. When they just won't let up. When they are spewing lies and persecuting you. But he waits. He waits on the Lord to come to intercede on his behalf. Waiting for God to deliver him. Praising Him the entire time. Not just praise, but overflowing praise.

The Psalmist gives us a great example to follow. If we never suffer we never learn to trust. We are to live according to His Word. To seek after Him with all of our heart. To keep His commands. We are to hide His Word in our hearts so we do not sin against Him. We are to rejoice in Him, meditate on His Word, filling your mind. Delight always in His ways. Strengthen us with Your Word when our souls are weary and full of sorrow. Pray for understanding of the Scriptures, keep them written on the tablets of your hearts so you can pull from them in times of need. May we always keep Your Word and truth upon our lips. We are free because of You, Lord. The Lord is our portion, forever. The earth is filled with His love. Teach us Your knowledge and good judgment. Help us to be compassionate to others. God is our refuge, our hiding place, and our shield. Direct our steps. Make Your face to shine on us.

Hope
"TO TRUST"

When trials come, and they will, what will others see in you? What you do matters. How you act and react matters. Having faith matters. Pray that others will see the Lord in you and rejoice. Because they see your faith. They see what God can and chooses to do in your life. They see your peace and your hope in a less than peaceful situation. Be the light for others. Be prepared to give the reason for the hope that you have. Be in constant prayer. God is here, He is faithful; He sees, and He knows. Place your trust and your hope in Him today.

Notes

Pray

We are

to protect

and

defend our

faith

HEBREWS 10:23

Let us hold unswervingly to the hope we profess, for he who promised is faithful.

Day 8

Hope
"TO TRUST"

In a young married class we were asked this question; "Do you think back in old testament times it was easier to sin than it is nowadays?" As a young wife and mother, I didn't quite grasp the concept of this question. However, it stuck with me and I'm not completely sure why. Years later, I finally have an answer. I believe it is easier to sin nowadays than it was in old testament times. My thoughts behind this are as follows. For one in old testament times if a person sinned they had to make a sin offering. Depending on the sin and its severity would depend on the animal used, typically one without blemish, their most valuable animal that they had. This living sacrifice had many rituals and rules surrounding it, and in offering up this living sacrifice they could make an atonement for their sins. Some as seen in Leviticus 20 carried a punishment of death. Other offerings that needed to be made were guilt and trespass offerings. With these, there were added damages that needed to be made along with the animal sacrifice. Furthermore, they didn't have direct access to God through Jesus.

Hebrews 1:4 says; *"It is impossible for the blood of bulls and goats to take away sins."* Jesus enters the picture. On the cross, Jesus broke through this barrier, the curtain. In fact, the curtain was torn from top to bottom immediately after the death of Jesus. Signifying entrance into the Holy of Holies. Jesus took on our punishments for our sins. He was our living sacrifice, the sacrificial lamb who was without blemish or spot. With Jesus, we are finally, truly forgiven. Our guilt washed away.

Because of this, we need to proclaim who Jesus is to all who will listen. We need to hold fast to who He is. We need to be grounded in our faith. Not allowing others to lead us one direction or another. We continually hold on to the hope of Jesus. Hold on to the trust that we have in Him. We are to protect and defend our faith. We are to have confidence in Jesus and His sacrifice for us. Our faith, our trust, our hope is something we should not hold on to lightly. Rest in Him today, hold fast to hope, because He is faithful.

Notes

We are

being

molded into

whom

Christ needs

us to be

1 Peter 5:10

And the God of all grace, who called you to His eternal glory in Christ, after you have suffered a little while, will Himself restore you and make you strong, firm and steadfast.

Day 9

Hope
"TO TRUST"

As Christians, we don't get a life void of trials. It's not a question of if, but when. Out of all of God's promises to us, having a trouble-free life was not one of them. James 1:2 says; *"Consider it pure joy, my brothers and sisters, whenever you face trials of many kinds,"*. John 16:33 Jesus tells us we will have tribulation. Romans 5:3 says to rejoice in our suffering. 1 Peter 4:12 says do not to be surprised when a fiery trial comes our way. In 1 Peter 1:6 he says *"In this you rejoice, though now for a little while, if necessary, you have been grieved by various trials,"* Attached to every one of these verses is hope, is learning, is life. Hope in what we can achieve through our trials. Hope in Jesus as He walks beside us in our trials.

As we all have gone through our own trials and tribulations we might ask how am I to rejoice when it hurts so bad? How can I rejoice when the suffering is long? How can I rejoice...? You fill in the blank.

Our trials are there to help guide us and to teach us if we are willing to learn. As I said before, if we never suffer, we never learn to trust. We can never fully understand the heart of God if we don't go through trying situations from time to time. The Scriptures tell us we rejoice because we know that this will bring about endurance. We learn how to process and move through our trials. Not as the world expects us to, but as God shows us to. Through our endurance, we gain character, and our character produces hope. Paul says that our hope does not put us to shame. We rejoice because our trials show the genuineness of our faith, and though being refined by fire, we praise, glory, and honor Jesus. We grow through our trials, we mature, gain wisdom, and our trials produce perseverance in us.

We are promised renewed strength, peace, provision, grace, mercy, and forgiveness when we follow closely after God. When we allow Him to do work on us and through us. We wait as God Himself restores us, He will make us strong, firm, and steadfast. In the midst of trials, we are being refined. We are being molded into whom Christ needs us to be. To fulfill our purpose and to bring God's hope to others.

So the next time you face a situation that brings you to your knees, rejoice. Rejoice in knowing that God is right there with you, holding you up, refining you, guiding you, loving you, comforting you, and restoring you.

Notes

Our hope

is in

Him alone

Yes, my soul, find rest in God; my hope comes from Him.

PSALM 62:5

Day 10

There is so much to learn from David. He had been through so much in his life. From being a Shepard boy, to being a skilled musician, to slaying Goliath. From being loved by King Saul to being hated by him, so much so King Saul wanted David dead. Oh, what jealousy can do to a person. And eventually becoming King. From his affair with Bathsheba to having her husband killed, being confronted by his friend, admitting his failures, repenting, asking God for forgiveness, being pursued many times by several people. From King Saul to his own son. David saw it all. He went from glory, honor, and wealth to hiding out in caves and back again.

David knew what it was like to live a life of abundance and a life of need. We see a recurring theme in David's Psalms. We see him cry out to the Lord about his suffering, and we see David proclaim God's goodness. Psalm 62 is no different. His soul finds rest in God. David was willing to wait on the Lord. Trusting in Him and His promises. Knowing that God was his fortress, his refuge, his hiding place. No matter what came towards David, he knew that with his faith in the Lord he would not be shaken.

David, a man after God's own heart, was also a sinner just like you and me. The one thing that we all have in common is being justified by God, forgiven of our sins. 1 Corinthians 6:11 says, *"And that is what some of you were. But you were washed, you were sanctified, you were justified in the name of the Lord Jesus Christ and by the Spirit of our God."* God has poured out His grace, mercy, and love to all of us.

God restored David many times. He gave David strength. Know this, God can and will do the same for you. Proclaim God to be your Lord and Savior. Know His love for you. Get to know His power and His promises. Our hope comes from the Lord. Our hope is in Him alone. He is our rock. Trust in Him today, sweet ones. Pray with me that you will find rest in God today. That your hope will forever come from Him. Stand firm in who you are and whose you are. Loved, strong, forgiven, full of hope, and so much more.

Notes

Silent prayers

reaching

their way

to God's

ears

And hope does not put us to shame, because God's love has been poured out into our hearts through the Holy Spirit, who has been given to us.

Day 11

B efore we get started, I just want to pause for a moment and say that I am struggling to find the words today. Not knowing where God wants to take me with this post. I am sitting here listening to worship music, which gets me going. Hands in the air oftentimes with tears streaming down my cheeks. Silent prayers reaching their way to God's ears. The sound, the words, they enter in like rolling thunder straight from heaven. The intensity and strength that it brings along with it is so powerful, you can feel it. Just like God's Word. His love. His hope. It wipes away any shame, any guilt, any repented sins. We are washed clean. Made white as snow. Cling to Him today, sweet ones. He is not letting go of you. Remember His promises. Remember that you are loved so fiercely. Remember who you are and whose you are.

God poured out His love into our hearts. God's love for us is woven throughout our entire bodies. Interconnected with Jesus, through the Holy Spirit. Hope does not put us to shame, other translations say hope does not disappoint. Our hope is rooted in who Christ is. Our hope in Christ is different from the world's hope. The world's hope is fleeting and can be disappointing. However, we are confident in our hope in God. God's hope is trust, a confident expectation in His promises. Trust in knowing that we are saved. A hope where we are allowed to rest. Can you imagine resting in Him so completely where shame and disappointment are no more?

You are more than your past. You are more than what was done to you. You are adopted in. A child of God. Set apart. You belong. You are loved.

Notes

God

entered in

Psalm 43:5

Why, my soul, are you downcast? Why so disturbed within me? Put your hope in God, for I will yet praise Him, my Savior and my God.

Day 12

My husband and I ran a small business together. We started out on top, flipped the industry on its ear. Brought about a change that was needed by so many. The problem was we were in a secular industry with a faith-based business. We didn't force our beliefs on anyone, but we didn't hide it either. As the years passed people saw what we had, saw what we were doing, and wanted it for themselves. The anger and hate towards us grew. They started to lie, big lies about our company and about who we were as people. I am not going to lie; it hurt. We were thrown for a loop. There were many times I said this verse in my prayers, *"Why my soul, are you downcast? Why so disturbed within me?"* Because they just wouldn't let up. Daily it seemed as if they were after us, pursuing us, gaining on us. Some days they pursued worse than others. Post after post, night after night. There were nights I sat in our bed and cried. There were nights I prayed for it all to go away. But I found hope and confidence in the Lord. He lifted us up. He provided for us despite the movement against us. We prevailed to the dismay of our pursuers.

God entered in. He made a way where there should have been no way. We took this opportunity to pray for those who were persecuting us. I even told our daughter many times, *"Well, this just gives me an opportunity to pray for them."* Matthew 5:44 says; *"But I tell you, love your enemies and pray for those who persecute you,"* We took the opportunity to lean on the Lord in our time of struggle. The Scriptures tell us in Psalm 37:7 to *" Be still before the Lord and wait patiently for him; do not fret when people succeed in their ways, when they carry out their wicked schemes."* The MSG translation says it this way "Quiet down before God, be prayerful before him. Don't bother with those who climb the ladder, who elbow their way to the top." This is what they were doing. They were trying to elbow their way to the top. It didn't matter to them who might get hurt in the process. They had their sites on tearing us down, regardless of the destruction it could have left in their wake.

But God, God wasn't phased by these people. He was faithful to us throughout the entire process. Our trust and our hope in God far outweighed their words, their lies, and their threats. We grew in hope; we grew in faith; we grew in our confidence in the Lord. All the while praising Him for His blessings. Praising Him for who He is, My Savior and my God.

Notes

Let's wait

in a

state of

hope and

trust

*WE WAIT IN HOPE FOR THE LORD; HE
IS OUR HELP AND OUR SHIELD.*

Day 13

Hope

"TO TRUST"

The Psalmist opens Psalm 33 with singing praises to the Lord. He continues with how mighty and powerful, and how great God is. He speaks of God's faithfulness and love. He reminds us that with a word God made the heavens. God speaks and things come to be, He commands and they stand firm. He reminds us that God is watching, He sees, He knows, He formed every one of our hearts. The Psalmist is praising God for all that He has done and all that He will do. And then we wait. We wait for God to move. We wait for God to do His work in the world, in us, and in those around us.

Have you noticed that waiting is hard? Waiting on that promotion. Waiting for marriage. Waiting for a baby. Waiting for the right guy you know God has planned for you. Waiting for an answer to a question asked, but not really wanting to hear the answer. Waiting for an answer to prayer. Waiting.

Often while we wait, if we allow, God will do a work in us. We should prayerfully look at what we are waiting for, but we should also prayerfully look internally at what God is teaching us. What is God trying to say to me? What do I need to work on in myself? What am I to learn through all the waiting? Because the time spent in the waiting is not a waste. We should cherish it. I think we sometimes miss out on what God has to offer us, the blessings that He will pour out if we just waited. We pray to God, but do we ever sit back and wait or listen? Wait for His response to our situation. Wait for His response to our prayers.

Waiting is hard. Especially when it is something that we have prayed so hard and so long for. But God is always right on time. Not our timing, but His. He works differently than we do. His timeframe differs from ours. The Psalmist finishes Psalm 33 with this; *"We wait in hope for the Lord; He is our help and our shield. In Him our hearts rejoice, for we trust in His holy name. May Your unfailing love be with us, Lord, even as we put our hope in You."*

Let's wait differently than we have in the past. Let's wait with anticipation and expectancy. Let's wait in a state of hope and trust. Knowing that God is there, lifting us up. Knowing that He will give us the rest we need. But within the waiting, let's not forget to move forward. Let's not forget that we still need to do the work, whatever that work might be. Let's do things differently as we move forward, knowing who God is. Hope, trust, peace, all placed in Him.

Hope
"TO TRUST"

Let's pray this over ourselves today. As we wait in hope, in trust for You Lord, knowing all the while You are our refuge and our hiding place, our shield in times of trouble. We rejoice in You and all that You have done. We rejoice in Your promises and in Your Word. We trust Your holy name and we thank You Lord for Your unfailing love. We place our hope in You today. Amen.

Notes

Pray

Faith

is the

foundation

of our

hope

HEBREWS 11:1

NOW FAITH IS
CONFIDENCE IN WHAT
WE *hope* FOR

AND ASSURANCE
ABOUT WHAT
WE DO NOT SEE

Day 14

Hope
"TO TRUST"

The writer of Hebrews, long believed to be Paul, spends chapter 11 of Hebrews talking about faith. The faith needed to walk through life and the different obstacles they faced. He speaks of Noah, Abraham, Isaac, Jacob, Joseph, Moses, and more. By faith, each sentence starts. Faith to hear God speak, faith to take action on what God said. And trust to bring it all to fruition. Trust in knowing that God would guide their steps. Lead them to where they needed to go. To provide for them along the way. All with one catch, a catch we don't have. They did not see or receive what was promised, Jesus Christ. Hebrews 11:13 says, *"All these people were still living by faith when they died. They did not receive the things promised; they only saw them and welcomed them from a distance, admitting that they were foreigners and strangers on earth."* Each lived by faith, each reached their God-given destination. Because they allowed God head over their lives and lived by faith, God was faithful. Each of them knowing that following the path God laid out for them would not be easy. It was going to be met with challenges along the way. But they marched forward anyway.

All of this culminates in Hebrews 11:1 *"Now faith is confidence in what we hope for and assurance about what we do not see"* They were confident in God. They had faith in God. They hoped in God.

If we can learn anything from these people, it is what faith in action looks like. Without the hands-on knowledge of Jesus Christ. But instead, the promises of God for Him. They knew someone was coming. They knew that they were not of this world.

Faith is the foundation of our hope. We find our confidence and sweet assurance within. We cannot always see what God is up to. But our faith knows that He is working. We have firsthand knowledge and the privilege of Jesus' teachings.

Continue to move forward in faith today. Even when it's hard. Because God is there. Paving the way. Providing for your every need. By faith, with hope, in peace.

Notes

Remember
that God
collects
all of your
tears in a
bottle

Romans 5:3-4

Not only so, but we also glory in our sufferings, because we know that suffering produces perseverance; perseverance, character; and character, hope.

Day 15

Hope
"TO TRUST"

Early morning as you are waking, the phone rings. The news is earth shattering. The death of a loved one taken far too soon. A discovery you wish you never found, one that left you curled up in a ball on the floor. The lies of someone closest to you crash over you like waves in a storm. A phone call in the afternoon the person on the other end says "We need to talk." Their admission breaks your heart, which leaves the pieces of your life scattered all over the floor. You find yourself with your cheeks flushed and hot to the touch. You can feel the warmth of your tears as they fall from your eyes. Your shoulders slowly moving up and down to the rhythm of your tears. Life, life has rushed in with a force you were not ready for.

But God, God bent down, He lifted you up into His arms and He held you. He comforted you. He gently wiped your tears from your eyes and whispered, *"My grace is sufficient for you, for my power is made perfect in weakness."* 2 Corinthians 12:9. *"So do not fear, for I am with you; do not be dismayed, for I am your God. I will strengthen you and help you; I will uphold you with my righteous right hand."* Isaiah 41:10.

Remember that God collects all of your tears in a bottle. Psalm 56:8. When we struggle and go through trials we are often heartbroken, hurt, in pain, and yearning for relief to come. But through our trials, our struggles, we can learn. If we allow we will let God do a work in us. The redemptive work of God moving through you. The peace that is in the pit of your stomach that shouldn't be there within your circumstances. But knowing that this peace, this hope, is from God alone. No other explanation. Peace and hope welling up within you even as your tears fall.

Through our sufferings, it produces perseverance, the ability to continue forward despite the difficulty. It develops our character, and it strengthens our hope. We know that we can fully trust in You God and understand that You will use it for our good and the good of others. As we grow and learn and hope this will eventually pour out to others who ask why do I have this hope.

"Consider it pure joy, my brothers and sisters, whenever you face trials of many kinds, because you know that the testing of your faith produces perseverance." James 1:2–3.

Notes

We will

experience

His

peace

Titus 3:7

so that, having been justified by His grace, we might become heirs having the hope of eternal life.

Day 16

Hope
"TO TRUST"

When we are justified we are declared, or made righteous in the sight of God, forgiven. Not by our own works, but through God's gift to us by grace through faith. We just have to be willing to accept His grace. Acknowledge and believe that Jesus is the Son of God and that He died on the cross for our sins. Our hope, and our trust, is in knowing that we will live in eternity in the presence of God. If you haven't already, are you willing to accept the free gift of salvation?

There is a process, but it's instantaneous. Let me explain. Everyone has the opportunity to be saved. You first accept God's free gift of salvation. Once you have accepted God's free gift of salvation you are adopted in. Once you are adopted in, you are God's child, until then you are God's creation. Once you are God's child you become co-heirs with Christ. The moment you accept Jesus Christ as your Lord and Savior, you become all of these. Your life will then benefit from God's grace. His mercy. Forgiveness of sins. His promises. His comfort. We will experience His peace. We will overflow with hope and trust in Him. Seek after Him today. Seek after Him every day. Make Him a priority in your life.

Bible verse references:
Opportunity - Romans 1:20
Free gift - Romans 6:23
Saved - Romans 10:9
Adopted in - Ephesians 1:5
God's child - Galatians 4:7
Co-heirs with Christ - Romans 8:17

Notes

And what

sweet

hope it is

"BUT NOW, LORD, WHAT DO I LOOK FOR? MY *hope* IS IN YOU.

PSALM 39:7

Day 17

Hope
"TO TRUST"

How many of you have found yourself in a place where you wanted to speak out? Where people were standing right in front of you, or perhaps in this day and age, someone speaking online, but they were not speaking the truth, coming after you, or maybe even after someone you know and love. You wanted to respond but knew it best to remain quiet. Knowing that if you spoke it wouldn't matter what was said. They would hear what they wanted to hear.

In Psalm 39 we see David nearing his wits' end with remaining silent. His response, in my opinion, was throwing his hands towards the heavens, in a desperate plea to the Lord. He said, *"But now, Lord, what do I look for?"* v.7. Other translations say *"what do I wait for"*. As if to say, why am I remaining quiet? How long Lord do I have to wait for You to say move? How long, Lord, what is it exactly that I am waiting for? Am I waiting for my enemies to tire and retreat? Am I waiting for the right words of wisdom to appear on my lips? Even then Lord I am afraid to speak. *"So I remained utterly silent, not even saying anything good."* v.2.

But David didn't stop there. He continued, *"My hope is in You"* v.7. And what sweet hope it is. David trusted in the Lord to guide his steps. He trusted in the Lord to give him the wisdom that he lacked. David remembered, or better yet, he reminded himself of God's goodness.

Let's claim this as our reminder of who God is. Let's claim God's hope in every circumstance that we face. He is good. He is faithful. He is true. God walks before you, guiding you every moment of your day.

Notes

I will

hope in

You

always

As for me, I will
always have
hope;
I will praise You
more and more.

PSALM 71:14

Day 18

O h Lord, You have proven to me repeatedly just how much You love me. Your faithfulness in my life has surpassed even my greatest expectations. Despite what I have gone through, despite what I may go through, my eyes will always be focused on You. I will forever praise Your name. I will forever proclaim Your goodness to everyone I know. I will hope in You always.

This is my prayer for each one of you. I pray that you will see God's faithfulness and feel His love for you. I pray that God will surpass your greatest expectations and that you will praise Him in all things at all times. I pray that your eyes will be focused on Him and Him alone. I pray that you will hope in Him always. Because He cares for you.

God is our savior. He is our protector. He is the Alpha and Omega, the beginning and the end. He is just. He is grace. He is mercy. He is love, and He is our hope.

Notes

He

has called

you by

name

the faith and love
that spring from
the hope stored up
for you in heaven
and about which
you have already
heard in the true
message of the
gospel

Colossians 1:5

Day 19

The Gospel means good news. The good news of Jesus Christ. Knowing who He is. How He acts and reacts. How He loves. His promises and His teachings. All bound up deep within you. Ready for a moment's notice to draw from. And because you have heard the gospel, the good news, and you believe that Jesus is your Lord and Savior, through your faith you have been saved. Flowing from your faith is action. Action poured out in loving God and loving others. We are His hands and feet. God delights in us doing His will and showing others who He is.

Paul is acknowledging the church in Colosse. He has heard about them, their faith, and their love for others. He praises them for doing a good job. He prays for them, for knowledge and wisdom. *"We continually ask God to fill you with the knowledge of his will through all the wisdom and understanding that the Spirit gives"* Colossians 1:9. Knowing that knowledge brings about strength, God's strength, which brings about endurance and patience. Wrapped up in their knowledge, strength, endurance, and patience is joyful thanks. Thanks to God who has qualified them. *"being strengthened with all power according to his glorious might so that you may have great endurance and patience, and giving joyful thanks to the Father, who has qualified you to share in the inheritance of his holy people in the kingdom of light."* v.11-12.

Do you know that God has qualified you? He has called you by name. He has called you into His Kingdom. He has prepared you to do His work. Everything that you have ever gone through has been in preparation for where God needs you to be. Listen to the still small voice inside of you. This is God leading and guiding you. Trust in Him. The hope that you have is stored up for you in heaven. Eternal life in the presence of God.

Notes

Pray

BE JOYFUL IN
HOPE, PATIENT
IN AFFLICTION,
FAITHFUL
IN PRAYER.

ROMANS 12:12

Day 20

Tue and proper worship is when we offer our bodies as a living sacrifice. This is holy and pleasing to God. Paul gives us a beautiful example of love in action. He says that love is to be sincere. Hate evil. Cling to good. Devote yourselves to one another in love. Honor each other. Serve the Lord with fervor. Practice hospitality. Bless those who persecute you. Rejoice with those who rejoice and mourn with those who mourn. Do not be proud or conceited. Do not repay evil with evil. Do what is right. Live in peace, if possible within your ability. Do not take revenge. God will deal with them in His way, in His timing. Be joyful in hope, patient in affliction, faithful in prayer.

Wow and Amen. In the middle of Paul's explanation of true and proper worship and love in action, he explains to us how to be humble. Humble in service in the body of Christ. Working together to accomplish what God has placed before us, the great commission. To go out and make disciples of all nations. We have been sent on a mission. One we need to take on with great intention and care. As Jesus followers, we all have different gifts, each unique, but each one just as important as the next. If your gift is a gift of service, Paul says to serve. If your gift is a gift of teaching, Paul says to teach. If you have a gift Paul says to use it. Don't sit on it. Don't squander what God has gifted you. God gives us our gifts according to His grace. God has handpicked you. He has set a path before you. He chose you on purpose for a purpose. Identify your gift, cultivate it, pray over it, and move when God says move. Listen closely to His voice, to His promptings in your life. He will be with you every step of the way. He will guide you and lead you.

We are to be joyful in hope. Joyful in what God has set before us. Joyful in the process. Joyful in our circumstances, good or bad. Joyful in Him. Keeping our eyes constantly on Him.

We are to be patient in affliction. When it gets hard, we press forward. We don't back down. Because God is on our side. We continue to hold fast to hope. We continue to pray continually.

We are to be faithful in prayer. 1 Thessalonians 5:17 simply says *"pray continually"*. But it's not so simple. We sometimes forget that prayer should come first before anything else. Before we react before we respond before we move. Pray. Prayer not only allows us to open up and be honest with God, but it also helps center us. It helps us to put things into perspective, God's perspective. Prayer can be done anywhere, while you are doing laundry, cleaning the house, in your car, before bed. It's not all about physical posture, but it's all about your heart posture.

We are to live out our calling, our gift with joy, patience, and faith. Trust in Him today, sweet ones. Maintain joyful hope in Him. Be patient in affliction and be forever faithful in prayer.

Notes

Pray

Handpicked

by God

Himself

I PRAY THAT THE EYES OF YOUR HEART MAY BE ENLIGHTENED IN ORDER THAT YOU MAY KNOW THE HOPE TO WHICH HE HAS CALLED YOU, THE RICHES OF HIS GLORIOUS INHERITANCE IN HIS HOLY PEOPLE,

Ephesians 1:18

Day 21

In the first part of Ephesians 1, Paul is talking about us being chosen. We were chosen by God before the creation of the world. Predestined for adoption. Once we hear the gospel, and we believe, then we are marked with a seal which is the Holy Spirit. Just listen to this, *"And you also were included in Christ when you heard the message of truth, the gospel of your salvation. When you believed, you were marked in him with a seal, the promised Holy Spirit, who is a deposit guaranteeing our inheritance until the redemption of those who are God's possession—to the praise of his glory."* v.13-14. Guaranteeing our inheritance, which is eternity with the Lord. As I was reading this today, the beauty of it all hit me. The sheer amount of planning, the knowledge God has of who I am, of who you are. Of being known, fully known by God the Father.

If you have ever felt unseen, unknown, lonely, know this; You were chosen. Before you even came to be. You were chosen. Handpicked by God Himself. Predestined according to His plan, *"who works out everything in conformity with the purpose of his will,"* v.11.

Paul is praying that the eyes of our hearts may be well informed about who Jesus is and what He has done for us. Once we have the knowledge of who Jesus is, then we will know His hope.

Remember that you have a calling on your life. You are seen. You are known. You are not alone. God is faithful in His calling of you. He will not leave you alone in it. Learn, study, press in, pray, and pursue. The Scriptures say; *"Your word is a lamp for my feet, a light on my path."*

Let us always remember; *"May the God of hope fill you with all joy and peace as you trust in him, so that you may overflow with hope by the power of the Holy Spirit."* Romans 15:13

Notes

About the Author

Michele Arnold, wife, mother of 2, and Mmma (Grandma) to 1 (for now). In the midst of doting on her grandbaby, Michele runs a small business with her husband. Michele has written, taught, and facilitated Bible studies, one-day workshops, and simulcasts. She maintains and runs In His Grace Ministries webpage where you can find articles about faith, family, devotionals and so much more. Michele is passionate about family, leading, equipping and confirming women about who they are in Christ, following the Lord and His leading in her life and that of her family.

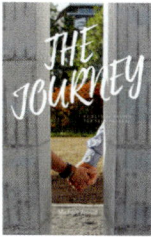

All throughout this devotional are ways to pray over, and for, your husband. We will delve into what it looks like being a wife and a woman of God and gain a better understanding of who we are in Christ. Let's consider some new thinking, based on timeless Biblical principles, contrasted against our current cultural and social norms. We have the life changing opportunity to gain a better understanding of how to move through your marriage and life in general, through God's lens. We have all gone through moments of great joys and deep pains. I pray that the words on these pages fill you with hope, peace, and a sense of who God is, and also, a sense of who you are in Christ.

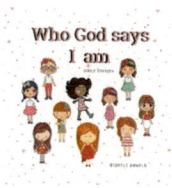

I am's are a positive affirmation of who your daughter is in Christ. A gentle reminder of her importance to Christ and the world. When we speak over our children about who they are in Christ they become equipped to handle what the world throws at them. The I am's give your daughters the confidence needed to pursue their calling and help them to know their true identity in Christ.

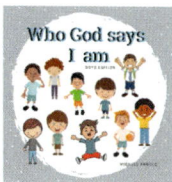

I am's are a positive affirmation of who your son is in Christ. A gentle reminder of his importance to Christ and the world. When we speak over our children about who they are in Christ they become equipped to handle what the world throws at them. The I am's give your sons the confidence needed to pursue their calling and help them to know their true identity in Christ.

Peace is a word we seem to use far and few between, but with God we can experience His peace every day. Even when our circumstances don't seem to align with peaceful feelings, you can be at peace in heart, soul, and mind. There truly is no greater feeling than being in complete peace. When we choose this peace, as God's free gift, we are set free and we are free indeed.

Journal Light for my path Bible study devotional takes on a unique perspective of your traditional Bible studies. Whether it be your first step in learning God's Word or you have been walking the path for some time, this is a great way to dip your toes into God's Word and who He is. This magazine is aimed at meeting the needs of young people transitioning in their faith from baby believers to maturing adults. Daily devotionals, creative space, and practical tools fill this magazine-style devotional for young people with a style relevant to their world.

Made in the USA
Middletown, DE
16 April 2022